The Kentucky Corn Cob Wine Connoisseur

By Jim Hubler
Author ~ Songwriter ~ Guitar Owner ~
Part-time Poet ~ Amateur Distiller

Produced by Hubler Enterprise/UNDUN
Records
Written by W.J. Hubler Jr., aka Jim Hubler
Book Design by Julie Curl
Copyright 2012 W.J. Hubler Jr.
All rights reserved.

Lightning Source®

Table of Contents

IN VINO VERITAS…

…is a Latin phrase that roughly translates to 'there is truth in wine'.
The reported author of the phrase is Pliny the Elder.

The Roman historian Tacitus described how the Germanic peoples "…always drank wine while holding councils, as they believed nobody could lie effectively when drunk".

Similar phrases exist across cultures and languages. In Chinese, there is the saying, "After wine blurts truthful speech".

The Babylonian Talmud contains the passage: "In came wine, out went a secret".

In the 1770s, Benjamin Cooke wrote a song by the title of *In Vino Veritas*. His lyrics [with modern punctuation, etc.] are as follows:

Round, round with the glass, boys, as fast as you can,
Since he who don't drink cannot be a true man.
For if truth is in wine, then 'tis all but a whim
To think a man's true when the wine's not in him.
Drink, drink, then, and hold it a maxim divine
That there's virtue in truth, and there's truth in good wine!

And here's another old Latin saying :
It is well to remember that there are five reasons for drinking: the arrival of a friend; one's present or future thirst; the excellence of the wine; or any other reason.

(Information in this section is from Wikipedia.)

PREFACE

"The Kentucky Corn Cob Wine Connoisseur", is the most complete and authoritative guide and reference on Kentucky corn cob wine and the proper usage and etiquette pertaining to this exquisite and most delightful beverage.

This book is expressly written for the 'adventurous wine buff', and certainly not for those with 'wimpy' taste buds.

This book is a 'must have', for the well informed wine aficionado, oenophile, and discriminating wine enthusiast.

This book would be the perfect gift for any 'self-ordained' wine authority.

DISCLAIMER: Please notice that we will not divulge the recipes, methods or secret ingredients for making 'Kentucky corn cob wine'. These are traditionally closely held family secrets, passed down from daddy to son for one helluva bunch of years.

Blabbing about these precious secrets could cause big trouble. If you don't know how to make Kentucky corn cob wine, you can find out how from books, magazines, and the Internet; or loose-mouthed people who blab about these precious secrets. We highly encourage you to develop your own corn cob wine recipe as an extension of your own unique personality.

This publication will only tell about this 'wondrous beverage', it's colorful history, wine etiquette, recommended wine/food pairings, proper labeling, ways to identify the genuine article from frauds and 'copycat' imitations, and more.

♥ ♥ ♥ ♥ ♥

KENTUCKY CORN COB WINE

DEFINITION AND BACKGROUND

- It's rougher than a cob, but it warms your innards.

- It's made in the hills of Kentucky by full blooded Kentuckians from a recipe passed down from daddy to son for one helluva bunch of years...nope, there ain't no use asking, you cain't have the recipe!

- While it is common knowledge that corn can be raised in most parts of the USA, as well as around most of the world, 'Kentucky corn' is far superior in taste and quality to most others. As well, this carries over to the corn cob, which is the most basic and vital ingredient in the highly skilled and delicate art of making 'Kentucky corn cob wine'.

Many claim that the near perfect blend of Kentucky sun and rain, fertile soil, and the waters found near, and even water from the Ohio River contribute to the excellence of Kentucky corn cob wine.

Some purists claim that using water taken directly from the Ohio River enhances the flavor and makes a more 'full bodied' wine. Other purists emphasize that water taken close to the Kentucky shore adds to the purity and sweetness of the wine.

For those that are picky over sanitation concerns, remember, we are located a fur piece downriver from Louisville and Cincinnati, so it's probably safe enough.

So, you see, much the same as how bourbon whiskey can only be labeled as bourbon when it's made with the waters from a certain place in Kentucky, how 'Florida grown' can only be applied to Florida grown oranges, and how 'Idaho potatoes' must be Idaho grown.

Thus you can see that it is with much pride in a product so steeped in tradition and history that we claim Kentucky corn cob wine to be very special.

We take much pride in carrying on these traditions. So, always look for the 'made in Kentucky label' to make sure you get the real deal. Also check to see that the bottle is carrying the following certification: 'made in the hills of Kentucky by full-blooded Kentuckians.

Be discriminating, accept no substitutes. There ain't nothing near as bad as a damn copycat, let's expose those who try to make counterfeit versions of this traditional beverage!

Remember…"You're living so fine, if it's Kentucky corn cob wine".

WINE TERMINOLOGY

Aficionado. A fan, or supporter, is a person with a liking and enthusiasm for something.

Appalachian. A native or resident living in the region around the Appalachian Mountains in Eastern USA.

Appellation. An appellation is a legally defined and protected geographical indication used to identify where the grapes for a wine were grown; other types of food often have appellations as well; an appellation name may legally appear on a wine bottle label. The rules that govern appellations are dependent on the country in which the wine was produced.

Aperitif. An alcoholic drink usually enjoyed as an appetizer before a large meal. It is often served with something small to eat, like olives or crackers.

Connoisseur. A person who has a great deal of knowledge about the fine arts, or an expert judge in matters of taste. The term connoisseur is also used in the context of gastronomy, i.e. in connection with fine food, beer, wine, tea and many other products whose consumption can be pleasing to the senses. Can easily be identified by their raised pinkie fingers when tasting pleasing beverages.

Dessert Wine. Sweet wines typically served with dessert. Despite the name, they are often best appreciated alone, or with fruit or bakery sweets.

Digestif. A beverage, usually small and alcoholic, which is drunk at the end of a meal. Bitter or carminative herbs are generally added to the alcohol, and some believe that such digestifs aid digestion, hence the name. Digestifs are usually drunk neat and are most often spirits, such as cognac, armagnacs, brandies, grappas, whiskies and herb flavored liqueurs. Some wines (usually fortified) may be served as digestifs, for example, port, sherry or madeira.

Enthusiast. 1.) One who is filled with enthusiasm; one who is ardently absorbed in an interest or pursuit. 2.) A zealot; a fanatic.

Full bodied. Adjective meaning having richness and intensity of flavor or aroma.

Horticulture. The science or art of cultivating fruits, vegetables, flowers, or ornamental plants.

Oenology (or enology). The study and making of wine.

Oenophile (or enophile). A lover or connoisseur of wines.

Sangria. Sangría is a wine punch typically from Spain and Portugal. The word *sangría* comes from the Spanish *sangre* meaning blood . It typically consists of:

- red wine,
- chopped or sliced fruit (often orange, apple, and/or peach; occasionally kiwi or banana),
- a sweetener such as honey or orange juice,
- a small amount of added brandy, triple sec, or other spirits.
- *gaseosa* (carbonated water).

Because of the variation in recipes, sangría's alcoholic content can vary greatly. The ingredients in sangría vary, particularly in the type of fruit used, the kind of spirits added (if any), and the presence or lack of carbonation.

White wine can be used instead of red, in which case the result is called *sangría blanca*. In some parts of southern Spain, sangría is called *zurra* and is made with peaches or nectarines. In most recipes, wine is the dominant ingredient and acts as a base. In some regions of Portugal, cinnamon is also added with the sweetener, so that it can spice up the flavor.

Preparation consists of cutting the fruit in thin slices or small cubes, then mixing in advance all ingredients except for ice and carbonated sodas. After several hours in a refrigerator to allow time for the fruit flavors to blend with the rest of the ingredients, the ice and any last-minute ingredients are added and the drinks are poured. In both Spain and Portugal, sangría is served throughout the country during summer, and around the year in the southern and eastern parts of the countries.

Sommelier. Also known as a wine steward, is a trained and knowledgeable wine professional, commonly working in fine restaurants, who specializes in all aspects of wine service as well as wine and food matching. The role is more specialized and informed than that of a wine waiter.

The principal work of a sommelier is in the areas of wine procurement, wine storage, wine cellar rotation, and expert service to wine customers. He's also the smarty-pants that brings the wine bottle to the table.

Vintage. 1.) The yield of wine or grapes from a vineyard or district during one season. 2.) Wine, usually of high quality, identified as to year and vineyard or district of origin. 3.) The year or place in which a wine is bottled.

Viticulture. The cultivation of grapes.

Vintner. A wine merchant. Also a synonym for winemaker. Also the feller that makes the corn cob wine.

Wafting. Smellin' the wine. Take a short sniff and waft the wine vapors into the nose rather then directly holding your nose over the opening of the glass. This don't mean snorting.

APPALACHIAN APPELLATION

While it is common knowledge that corn can be raised in most parts of the USA, as well as around most of the world, 'Kentucky corn' is far superior in taste and quality to most others. As well this carries over to the corn cob, which is the most basic and vital ingredient in the highly skilled and delicate art of making Kentucky corn cob wine.

Many claim that the near perfect blend of Kentucky sun, rain, fertile soil, and the waters found near, and even water from the mighty Ohio River contribute to the excellence of Kentucky corn cob wine.

Some purists claim that using water taken directly from the Ohio River enhances the flavor and makes a more 'full bodied' wine. Other purists emphasize that water taken close to the Kentucky shore adds to the purity and sweetness of the wine.

For those that are picky over sanitation concerns, remember, we are located a fur piece downriver from Louisville and Cincinnati, so it's probably safe enough.

So, you see, much the same as how bourbon whiskey can only be labeled as bourbon when it's made with the waters from a certain place in Kentucky, how 'Florida grown' can only be applied to Florida grown oranges, and how 'Idaho potatoes' must be Idaho grown.

Thus you can see that it is with much pride in a product so steeped in tradition and history that we claim Kentucky corn cob wine to be very special. We take much pride in carrying on these traditions. So always look for the 'made in Kentucky label' to make sure you get the real deal. Also check to see that that the bottle is carrying the following certification: 'Made in the hills of Kentucky by full-blooded Kentuckians, from a recipe passed down from daddy to son for one helluva bunch of years. Nope, there ain't no use asking, you cain't have the recipe.' Be discriminating, accept no substitutes.

There ain't nothing near as bad as a damn copycat, let's expose those who try to make counterfeit versions of this traditional beverage!

Remember, 'you're living so fine, if it's Kentucky corn cob wine"

CLASSIC EXAMPLES OF KENTUCKY CORN COB WINE LABELS

This ain't fruit of the vine,
it's fruit of the stalk.
Too much of this can
change how you walk.

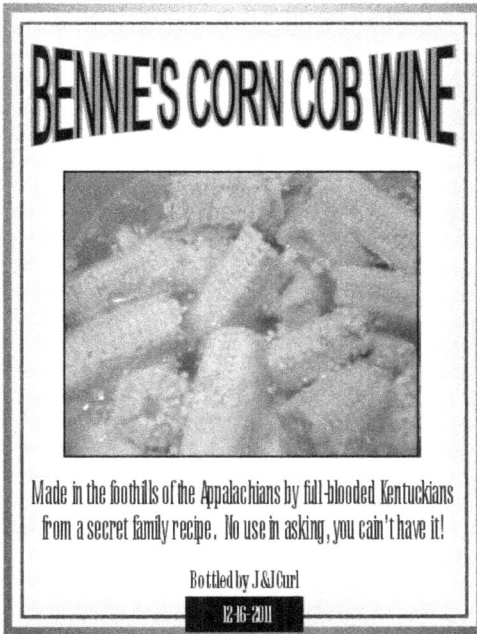

BENNIE'S CORN COB WINE

Made in the foothills of the Appalachians by full-blooded Kentuckians
from a secret family recipe. No use in asking, you cain't have it!

Bottled by J&J Curl

12-16-2011

Kentucky
Corn Cob Wine

Made in the hills of Kentucky by full-blooded Kentuckians. Recipe passed down from daddy to son for one helluva bunch of years. (Nope, there ain't no use asking - you cain't have the recipe!)

Jim Hubler
Master Distiller

August 2011

SOME PHRASES AND REMARKS PERTAINING TO KENTUCKY CORN COB WINE

What follows are but a few of the many slogans, phrases, and remarks seen on jugs, bottles, and mason jars of Kentucky corn cob wine…

> There is none so fine, as corn cob wine.

> Kentucky corn cob wine, it's rough as a cob but warms your innards.

> Kentucky corn cob wine, there's a giggle in every gulp.

> Tain't for wine snobs or sissies to swirl in a glass. Overdo on this stuff, it will kick your ass!

> If it's vintage wine, the wine drinker seeks, the time spent making this was over two weeks.

- Vintage: two of the best weeks in two-thousand nine. Of course that's why this wine tastes so fine.

- Our wine barely makes the trip to our cellar when it's being drank down by some thirsty feller.

- If you're thinking of having just a wine tasting, I really feel that it's time you are wasting.

- Please let me say, here's what I'm thinking - Y'all come on over, we'll have a wine drinking!

MIND YOUR MANNERS

Don't drink from the bottle.
Damn man, have some class!
Use a paper cup or even a glass.

Mind your manners,
Don't act like a hick.
Wipe your mouth with your sleeve, and please don't lick.

➢ This wine ain't for sipping, now try not to frown,
  Take a big gulp and swallow it down.

➢ We will bottle no wine, before it's time.
  We promise we never will.
  We call it Kentucky corn cob wine,
  But some folks call it 'swill'.

➢ Some claim corn cob wine tastes a bit brawny,
  In comparison other wines seem a bit scrawny.
  It's a full bodied wine, take it from me,
  It will boost up your spirits, try some you'll see.

➢ The taste of corn cob wine ain't easily forgotten.
  Some critics claim it tastes a bit rotten.
  We put corn cob wine in a blind taste test,
  And even the blind, judged it the best.

- Corn cob wine makes a bold statement, and to say the least it is 'loud-mouthed'.

- This moderately priced wine will speak to your wallet, in these times of economic austerity.
  Though its name is quite unbecoming,
  Its delight is right up among 'em!

- For the wine aficionado
  Just in case you care,
  Corn cob wine is not timid,
  One drink, you know it's there

- It's reputation precedes it,
  Some say it doesn't say enough.
  Some say it's a vivacious wine,
  Others say it's a tad bit rough.

- The perfect wine for the working man,
  When work's a little slack.
  Some drink it from the bottle,
  While some drink it from a sack.

➤ Not a real high-toned wine,
   Snobs drink with their pinkie raised,
   But in tasting after tasting,
   It has been highly praised.

➤ To find a drink this cheap, is
   exhilarating,
   It's nutritious and invigorating.

➤ A wine that's ready for 'prime time',
   And takes a back-seat to none,
   Is judged the best of all the rest.
   Try corn cob wine for drinkin' fun!

➤ Vitamin pills with corn cob wine,
   No matter if you're poor or wealthy,
   There is no doubt, you'll still get
   smashed,
   But at least you might stay healthy!

➤ Yet another exotic wine is born,
   It's made from a by-product of corn.
   An example of American ingenuity,
   Made for the likes of you and me.

➢ Corn cob wine is 'budget friendly',
  During times of economic austerity,
  If you can find the corn cobs,
  The wine is damn near free!

➢ This here corn cob wine ain't made for
  the meek.
  Just to make this brew took more than
  a week.
  Just chug it on down,
  And try not to frown.

➢ To think that corn cobs,
  Once considered throwaway stuff,
  Now are in a beverage,
  That tastes really tough.

➢ It's good vintage,
  Kentucky corn cob wine,
  Made back in the hills,
  Where the sun don't shine.

➢ A glass of this stuff,
  Puts a glow on your cheeks,
  The time took to make it
  Was over two weeks.

➤ It's a full-bodied wine,
   With an excellent bouquet.
   Though it's a bit impertinent,
   Some people say.

➤ Corn cob wine will quench your thirst.
   Forget the rest, try this one first.

REVIEWERS AND REVIEWS

SOME REMARKS AND CRITIQUES FROM WINE
TASTERS AND CRITICS:

> Lord Chauncey Drippingtool, noted
  English wine authority, made the
  following comments: "Kentucky corn
  cob wine is a full-bodied wine, with an
  excellent bouquet, though a bit
  impertinent, perhaps even damn
  impertinent! Yes, damn impertinent!"

> Another noted French wine
  connoisseur, Pierre the sensitive, had
  this to say: "As an experienced wine
  authority, I can't help but wonder what
  subtle characteristics this wine would
  have developed had its maker used all,
  or even part of the third week in its
  making."

> German wine reviewer, Heimlich
  Maneuver offered these comments:
  "The purchaser of this wine should be
  warned to not consume corn cob wine

in the close proximity of a pig pen, as it could very easily start a 'swine riot'."

California wine taster, Sherman Snobby, made these remarks: "One should be required to drink corn cob wine with the bottle still concealed in a brown paper bag so no one could see what was being consumed. Damn! It could take weeks for my delicate taste buds to recover."

Percival Pickeydude, noted British wine authority, remarked: "Good Lord, this is an abomination of fermentation! This drink is different from any I've seen. Hell, it borders on being obscene!"

One famous reviewer, who refused to be identified, made the following critical remarks: "This is nothing more than a wine-making abortion! Someone else can have my portion." He further said: "If my name is mentioned in connection with this event, I will deny every having been here!"

Another unidentified reviewer said: "This wine's subtleties and nuances are many. May I be excused if I don't drink any?"

One cranky wine critic said our Kentucky corn cob wine was a 'wine making atrocity'. I don't know for sure, but if I find out he was talking dirty, he's gonna be in big trouble!

Yet another wine critic, who said he would deny having ever participated, said our wine was one not easily forgotten. But did stop short of saying it tasted rotten.

One anonymous critic claimed corn cob wine flavor was a 'country taste so pure'. A powerful robust concoction for sure!

A noted wine critic from Texas made this observation: "To not try corn cob wine would be discrimination, so give it a try and you just might, learn to love this earthy delight."

A noted wine reviewer from Great Britain, was not impressed or even smitten, saying: "Chaps, it's a bit rough 'round the edges, perhaps they've inadvertently bottled some dredges. Perhaps corn cobs should be left for the swine, instead of trying to turn them to wine. Obviously it's what only commoners would buy, for a quickly obtained economical high."

➢ A noted Scottish beverage authority and reviewer, Angus McDermott made these comments: "Hoot mon, this beverage is a wee bit feisty! Yes laddies, it has somewhat of a Scottish personality, reminiscent of a highland fling! Yes, it's a frugal drink with humble origins but its flavor has some noble qualities - an honest drink at a bargain basement price. "

"You say Kentucky corn cob wine is made from the lowly corn cob? I'm thinking that the originator of this recipe most surely must have had Scottish roots."

➢ A Texas wine authority had this to say: "Whoopy ti yi, what a way to get a high. This drink is gutsy, with a lot of back sass, like you've been bucked from a bronco, that's after drinking only one glass. Yep pardner, when you're parched out riding the range, drink corn cob wine for a change."

➢ A well known Mexican critic, Manuel Feelwell said enthusiastically: "Ah, chihuahua, this el gringo corn cob wine is the answer to too much tequila. Ay caramba, is there no end to Americano ingenuity? If only we could grow more corn in Mexico! This Kentucky corn cob wine has a fiesta feel, señor. I do think this is the real deal!"

➢ An Italian wine critic said, unceremoniously: "When comparing corn cob wine to vino, there's really no contest, it's easy to see why hillbillies, like this stuff the best. If Michelangelo had been hitting on this, he might have had more fun, but the art in the Sistine Chapel never would have got done!"

➢ Another California reviewer said: "Corn cob wine has some earthy undertones. Now I don't want to sound mean or hard, but it could be said it tastes much like an old barnyard!"

➢ A famous writer/songwriter/wino, said the following: "This corn cob wine has many attributes, of which its maker should be proud – it's rather bold personality stands out in a crowd."

- Remarks by the famous British wine critic, Sir Cedric Blunt: "I want to say, right from the start, corn cob wine's not for the faint of heart!"

- A Boston wine critic said: "Here is the way it seems to me, here is my position. It's an unobtrusive wine crying for recognition."

- Well-known Georgia wine taster, Zeke 'Deliverance' River made these remarks: "It's a wine with a touch of Yankee back-sass, but even still, it has lots of class. It would be the right wine, if y'all don't over-do, on a north Georgia river, in a canoe."

- British wine authority, Sir Cecil Glutton said: "This wine tends to be a bit unsophisticated, perhaps its maker's parents were related!"

- Yet another Texas wine authority, Hop-along Capacity said: "Yup, it's plain another fine wine's been born, it's sorta like being gored by a mean Longhorn."

> **One wine reviewer's remarks:** "It is indeed gratifying to see that someone's ingenuity has found a way for the humble corn cob, which formerly was found to be useful only in rural outhouses, to be used in such a refreshing beverage to be enjoyed by the masses.

Undoubtedly, this is just another example of American ingenuity and bold thinking. With thinking like this, we are bound to remain a world power."

➤ As for 'aftertaste', at a wine fest last fall, one critic said after tasting, he could taste nothing at all!

➤ Big Daddy Cool, a noted New York City wine critic, said the following: "Corn cob wine is not dull, or droll. 'Bro', this wine is truly rock and roll!"

🌽 🌽 🌽 🌽 🌽

ETIQUETTE AND SERVING TIPS

PROPER ETIQUETTE (MIND YOUR MANNERS) WE
LIVE IN A CULTURED CIVILIZED SOCIETY

SOME SUGGESTIONS FOR SERVING KENTUCKY
CORN COB WINE PROPERLY:

➢ Once you take the cork from the
bottle, throw the damn thing away. It's
easier to drink it all down than to put
the cork back in.

➢ Passing the bottle of corn cob wine
around and drinking from the bottle is
not recommended. It looks damn
uncouth, and is said to be an unsanitary
practice. However, if you do participate
in this bottle-passing drinking, at least
wipe your mouth on your shirt sleeve
before and after drinking. It's only
good manners to do so.

Always try to keep your pinkie finger
raised, a universal sign of good
breeding. After all, we don't want

people thinking we are uncultured hicks.

- ➤ Remember, the well mannered guest should always offer the host serving the corn cob wine, a compliment of some sort. For instance, after wafting in (smelling) the excellent bouquet of the wine, and commenting on its nuances and subtleties, perhaps one could say, "Excellent corn cob wine, that was a very good two weeks."

- ➤ We encourage you to drink responsibly. This means holding the jug, bottle, or jar firmly with both hands. Drop the damn thing and you may have to clean up the mess your own self. Besides that, it could endanger the environment and result in the necessity for an in-depth environmental cleanup by the EPA, or OSHA, or one of them.

🌽 🌽 🌽 🌽 🌽

WINE AND FOOD PAIRINGS

FOR GOURMET GASTRONOMICAL DELIGHT, MAKE
SURE YOUR WINE AND FOOD PAIRING IS RIGHT.

Kentucky corn cob wine goes well with
most food, especially when in an
adventurous mood. Some suggestions:

> I might suggest, for a gourmet delight,
  Try it with hog jowls and grits this very
  night.
  For a gastronomical delight, to make
  spirits rise,
  Try corn cob wine with 'Spam® Surprise'.

> For a 'down home favorite', with a
  touch of class, try corn bread and beans
  with corn cob wine in a glass.

> It has long been claimed, as an appetite
  whetter, corn cob wine makes damn
  near anything taste better!

> Kentucky corn cob wine is excellent when paired with 'possum pizza', truly a gourmet delight.
> Get classy and try this wine and pizza tonight.

♥ ♥ ♥ ♥ ♥

WINE AND CHEESE PAIRINGS

BRING OUT THE BEST OF
BOTH

SOME SUGGESTED
PAIRINGS OF CORN COB
WINE AND CHEESES BY
AN EXPERT IN THE
FIELD

➤ **Highly recommended:** Kentucky corn cob wine and Cheese Whiz®. The excellent delicate flavors of each seem to complement each other; the subtle flavor of corn cob wine enhancing the delightful flavor of the Cheese Whiz®.

➤ **Less exotic, but never the less, well worth trying:** Kentucky corn cob wine and Velveeta® cheese. For an added gourmet touch, include Ritz® crackers.

➢ **Worth noting:** Several cheeses that are included in the US Government Surplus Food Commodity Program do pair up very well with Kentucky corn cob wine. However at the time of this writing, I am reluctant to suggest any of these, since I have not actually tasted them.

As a wine and food authority, I have my reputation to think of!

ABOUT BOTTLE CAPS AND CORKS

There seems to be an ongoing controversy between those who prefer capped bottles versus those with corks.

While it's true some do get their jollies with a cork and corkscrew, there's no doubt about it there are quite a few.

As well, other folks prefer plain old bottle caps.

Due to numerous requests, we are now sealing some bottles with corks, for some of our most discriminating clientele. We ask you to please remember that it costs about a quarter more to use a cork, versus a bottle cap.

Please try to remember, that if you are gonna act like a 'high rolling heavy', it's gonna cost more. Yep, it's an extra quarter if you want a cork, so don't bitch at us over this!

Furthermore you are gonna have to invest in a corkscrew, 'cause a pocket knife just won't do.

Taken from the wine list of Commander's Palace Restaurant in New Orleans, LA:

Here's to the corkscrew - a useful key to unlock the storehouse of wit, the treasury of laughter, the front door of fellowship, and the gate of pleasant folly.

PATRIOTISM AND CIVIC-MINDEDNESS

In these austere economic times, during the financial struggles the current administration in the USA is facing, I respectfully offer this helpful suggestion. In the interest of easing our nation's current budgetary problems, I suggest that Kentucky corn cob wine be served at all dinners, banquets and social functions at the White House.

There is no drink more American than Kentucky corn cob wine. We all know grape wines are often of foreign origin. Let's cut down on the outsourcing. After all, it is a tribute to American ingenuity that Kentucky corn cob wine can be made from the lowly corn cob, which was once thought only useful in the outhouse; now it can be served and enjoyed at the White House.

Indeed, I think this an excellent parallel.

🌽 🌽 🌽 🌽 🌽

VERSATILITY OF AND VARIOUS USES FOR CORN COB WINE

AS A 'BRACER', EARLY IN THE DAY: It can get you up and going.

AS A BEFORE DINNER DRINK; OR AN APERITIF: Excellent! A few gulps of Kentucky corn cob wine before a meal makes damn near anything taste better. Fer shore, it will whet your appetite.

AS A DRINK WITH YOUR MEAL: Very good, highly recommended! What with all of the corn cob wine's capabilities of fighting against harmful bacteria and such, now coming from cross-border food shipments.

AS AN AFTER DINNER DRINK, 'A DIGESTIF', OR, AS SOME CALL IT, 'DESSERT WINE': Again very good! It's said by some to be an excellent aid to digestion. As well, a few glasses of corn cob wine will make even the most droll or boring after-dinner speaker seem better. You might even laugh at his jokes!

AS A 'RELAXER': Again, an excellent choice. Some claim that after a few gulps they can sleep uninterrupted 'til time for morning chores.

AS A 'NIGHT-CAP', OR SLEEP AID: Kentucky corn cob wine is an excellent alternative to hot chocolate. It's organic, home grown, and contains no preservatives or none of that stuff.

AS AN AID AGAINST WORRY, NERVOUS TENSION, OR DEPRESSION: Many claim that while imbibing an adequate amount of Kentucky corn cob wine, you wouldn't care if Fidel Castro got elected to the Oval Office.

Others recommend just the right combination of Kentucky corn cob wine and 'Mexican laughing tobacco' to obtain the desired effects.

We don't recommend this, but it's all a matter of personal choice.

AS AN ANTISEPTIC FOR MINOR FIRST AID, IN EMERGENCIES ONLY: Some claim Kentucky corn cob wine should be included in all first aid kits, and medicine cabinets. Just apply liberally to the affected area. Also, a few swigs or swallows can act as a pain killer.

FIRST AID FOR ANIMALS: Yes, very good for dogs, horses, and mules. But a few words of caution – take care when applying Kentucky corn cob wine too liberally to injured areas of horses and especially your mule. That is, areas where the animal can lick the treated area. YOU MIGHT HAVE TO WALK HOME ALONE!!

COOKING WITH CORN COB WINE

Word is out that more and more gourmet chefs are discovering the many benefits of using this wine in their exotic recipes.

It is said to work very well in 'road kill' recipes, and enhances the flavor of most entrees.

Famous German chef, Heinreich Messmaker, has started using Kentucky corn cob wine in his recipes, and says: "Javohl and danke schoen to the makers of corn cob wine!"

Whether used by the common fry cook or celebrity chef, or the gastronomical adventurer, it makes food different for sure.

For a true culinary delight, include corn cob wine in your recipe tonight.

PAIRING THE RIGHT HORS D'OEUVRES

Meat: In this department, some say that corn cob wine with Vienna sausages is an excellent go together. Others have recommended bologna as an excellent match. However, care should be taken to only use the very best "premium bologna" as to not cheapen the occasion.

Peanut Butter: Another good hors d'oeuvre and Kentucky corn cob wine pairing is peanut butter laden celery sticks. Again, take care to use only the best peanut butter. For the sake of appearance, if using US Government Commodity peanut butter at least tear the label from jar to avoid your guests starting unflattering rumors about your financial condition.

Fried Green Tomatoes: Yet another great go-together in this department is fried green tomatoes and Kentucky corn cob wine. Though this may sound somewhat unorthodox, these two complement each other well.

Fried Dill Pickles: See above.

Seasonal Fruit: also, at least two other exotic but seasonal fruits work well with corn cob wine. They are namely, persimmons and paw paws.

When serving an hors d'oeuvre such as these, it's obvious to all present that you have definitely 'arrived'. As well, a vital part of the game is 'keeping up appearances', class to the max!

ONE UPLIFTING THOUGHT

The possible economic impact of Kentucky corn cob wine is great and should not be overlooked!

The discovery and popularity of Kentucky corn cob wine could very well be the answer to a wino's prayers. And as well could well have an impact on our stagnate economy.

If the largely homeless winos on the streets of America's largest cities were to start loving the taste of this delicious beverage as well as its affordability, they might want to start making corn cob wine. This in turn could very well encourage them to migrate to the central corn belt and rural regions of our country, primarily to have easy and more economical access to corn cobs to use in the wine making. Were this to happen, this could well be a great relief to our larger cities' welfare budgets.

Yes, this could be a boon to our sagging economy!

CORN COB WINE COCKTAILS

Now that you have been thoroughly educated about Kentucky corn cob wine and the things pertaining to it, there is more to be learned. There are several other uses for corn cob wine; the following are but a few of them.

Wines have a long history of use in mixed drinks of all kinds, here are a few. Again, we encourage you to be innovative, creative, inventive, bold and adventurous.

THE MOUNTAIN MANHATTAN

A NEW TWIST TO AN OLD FAVORITE

There are many variations of the drink called a Manhattan. It is traditionally whiskey or booze of one kind or another, some wine, typically vermouth, and usually garnished with a maraschino cherry. Yes indeed, a high class drink.

Now, here's a 'poor man's' version, said to be common in parts of the back-country. It contains three parts of a corn drink, produced back in the hills, then two parts Kentucky corn cob wine, usually garnished with a persimmon. Swizzle sticks are seldom used; some stir with a finger, while some use a pocketknife.

THE WINE COOLER

WINE COOLERS ARE QUITE POPULAR NOWADAYS

A variation of this is a 'wine fooler', made with Kentucky corn cob wine and various other ingredients. It is also aptly called 'wine surprise'. There are many creative versions of this type of drink.

And let's not forget the several lemonade drinks of today. A Kentucky favorite is 'laughing lemonade'. It is said to be a special blend of traditional lemonade and liberal amounts of Kentucky corn cob wine. This beverage is said to be very popular among ladies aid groups, and the like.

CORN COB WINE SANGRIA

HISTORY OF KENTUCKY CORN COB WINE SANGRIA

Kentucky corn cob wine sangria, often called 'el gringo sangria' by our Latino friends, is a delicious beverage and has long been a favorite in these parts.

First off, here is the basic history of this drink as it pertains to this part of the country. It has long been traditionally rumored that sangria making was started in these parts back about 1846, during the Mexican War.

Some of our Kentuckian troops went down to Mexico to fight General Santa Anna after that the Alamo battle. It wasn't long 'til some of our ever-thirsty soldiers discovered that them Mexicans was making one damn good beverage which they called sangria.

Some of our Kentuckian troops brought back the basic recipe for making sangria with them. Subsequently, they developed their own 'interpretation' of sangria, basing it not on grape wine, but using traditional and readily available Kentucky corn cob wine, local fruits, and some other delightful secret ingredients.

ULTIMATE RED NECK SANGRIA

This delightful creation is the result of intensive research and experimentation and very discriminating taste tests by experienced professionals. After long hours in our blending cellar, we are proud to present this superb sangria for the drinking pleasure of our discriminating clientele.

 It is a masterful blend of Kentucky corn cob wine, persimmons and paw paws, with just a hint of the exotic essence of sassafras. However, the rest of this masterful recipe is a secret combo of exotic herbs and spices only commonly found in the hills of this part of Kentucky.

The last, a key ingredient list, is a closely held secret in these parts and has been handed down from daddy to son for one helluva bunch of years; nope, no need in asking.

As is traditional for those who make sangria, there are many and varied recipes and formulas for the concoctions.

In many countries there are on-going friendly competitions among those who make sangria. We encourage you to try your hand at making your own unique blend. Of course, we recommend using genuine Kentucky corn cob wine as the base for the sangria.

It has been said that our style of sangria is made by 'rednecks' that only turn their cap bills backward when they work on their trucks.

Very probably this remark was made by traditional 'wine snobs'. No doubt, they were jealous of our beverage crafting skills.

SOME OF THE LABELS SEEN ON THE SANGRIA
CREATIONS ARE:

➤ Redneck sangria

➤ Gringo sangria

➤ El gringo sangria

➤ El gringo fiesta sangria, mas fina,
  especial

➤ Tailgater's sangria, and as well, by many
  other names.

REVIEWERS' COMMENTS ABOUT REDNECK SANGRIA:

Noted Tex-Mex sangria authority, Felipe Feelgood said the following:
"Ay caramba, if too many Mexicans learn of this luscious sangria, they'll be coming north in great numbers! Kentuckian sangria makers, you got it right amigos!"

Hispanic sangria authority, Jiminez 'The Guzzler' Garcia said the following: "What an innovative use for corn, which my people previously thought of as only being good for making tortillas, tacos, fajitas and so on. In my expert opinion, I judge 'el gringo red neck sangria as charming, elegant and very pleasing to the palate."

Yet another sangria authority from south of the border, Manuel 'The Thirsty Hombre', said: "My northern neighbors, your innovative interpretation of traditional sangria is 'mas fina', muchas gracias muchachos! We had no clue you could improve on an already great beverage".

Pedro Perales, Mexicano wine authority said, "Santa Maria, here is what I think, corn cobs from Kentucky make an especial drink."

Rafael Ramiriz, professor and sangria critic from Mexico City made the following comments, "Here is how it seems to me – it's one aggressive beverage, high in volatility."

AND YES, THERE'S MORE ABOUT ANOTHER SANGRIA FORMULATION:

A recently developed variation of 'el gringo red neck sangria is truly an 'enhanced version' of the former. It is aptly named, 'el gringo high test fiesta sangria'. It is also known to some hombres as, 'el gringo high test fiesta mas fina especial'. It is said to contain some additional corn products obtained from discreet producers who reside farther back in the hill country.

It is rumored to be a favorite drink of Mexican matadors who dare to face bulls head-on.

Some say this drink will damn shore wet your whistle! Andele! Arriba! Santa Maria! Ay chihuahua! As a cautionary note, it is thought to be unsafe to light cigarettes or cigars or use any open flame too close to this volatile concoction.

ENVIRONMENTAL ASPECTS OF THIS BEVERAGE

If you are into the 'green thing' organic, eco-friendly, and all of that, Kentucky corn cob wine is certainly all of these in every respect.

Upton Sinclair wrote in his book, 'The Jungle', that "'they (the meatpacking industry) use everything about the hog except the squeal."

Well consider this; people and livestock eat corn, cows eat the stalks as fodder or silage, and yet other enterprising people like us make delicious corn cob wine from the cobs. So, it can be said, "Unlike processing hogs, using all but the squeal,

You recapture it all from corn, including the 'feel'."

And you can even recycle the Kentucky corn cob wine bottles by making your own bottle tree! What is a bottle tree? Read on.

The bottle tree reflects an ancient African

tradition that can be traced as far back as ninth century Congo where natives hung hand-blown glass on huts and trees to ward off evil. The tradition continued in Africa and eventually became a part of Southern African-American folklore. In the early American South, trees, typically cedar because its branches point toward the heavens, were stripped of foliage and decorated with colorful glass bottles.

According to African legend, the bottles attract evil spirits, which are drawn to the bursts of sunlit color. The spirits then become trapped inside the bottles, their voices heard moaning as the wind passes by. Though the legend that the bottles trap evil spirits is widely accepted, some believe that the bottles hold the spirits of their ancestors, while others contend that the bottle tree grants wishes.

(Bottle tree information from "The Campus Chronicle", Savannah College of Art and Design. Photograph from Wikipedia Commons.)

Note: Kentucky corn cob wine poses no environmental waste problems and is 'wildlife friendly' for the following reasons:

- When you dispose of the leftover sludge from making the wine, the 'coons, possums, rabbits, and squirrels in the woods have an enjoyable time, thus - 'wild life friendly'.

- There have even been accounts of stray dogs partying down, which in these parts gives a whole new meaning to 'party animal'.

- When you observe some of the woodland birds diving at your truck like WWII kamakazi planes, while singing at the top of their lungs, perhaps they too may have been taking part in the 'wildlife happy-hour'.

However, as an addendum, I do feel obliged to relate the following accounts relating to the disposal of the leftover sludge from Kentucky corn cob wine making. All stories relating to the discarded wine-making sludge do not necessarily have a happy ending.

OTHER HOMEMADE SPIRITS

THEODORE TOMCAT

A rural parish priest, Father Flannigan
realized that his church was on a limited
budget. He noticed that the cost of the
communion wine used in his church was
growing more expensive. So, he decided to
economize by making and using Kentucky
corn cob wine for church, as well as
personal use.

Father Flannigan had a cat named
Theodore Tomcat. For years, Theodore
had terrorized the local field mice, and
showed them no mercy. However, the
tables soon turned. Shortly after Father
Flannigan had disposed of some leftover
corn cob wine sludge in the woods,
Theodore Tomcat returned late from his
usual 'field mouse expedition'.

Theodore obviously had suffered a terrible
experience in the woods. He had two black
eyes, a swollen cheek, and numerous

patches of cat hair missing about his body. Though shaken and in pain, Theodore Tomcat did survive and slowly hobbled home.

A witness, a local forester, said he came upon the scene by chance, and told the following story.

It appeared that a large group of field mice had 'partied down' on the leftover corn cob wine sludge. Instead of feeling giggly and happy, they felt inclined to fight.

When Theodore Tomcat came on the scene to brutalize the field mice as usual, he got a rude surprise. The drunken field mice overwhelmed Theodore and gave him a sound thrashing that he would not soon forget. He escaped with his life, but learned a much needed lesson.

Sometimes drunken parties are not all grins and giggles. The next two stories are accounts of various different 'impromptu' spirited beverages. These accounts are unusual and quite unique and we feel they need to be publicized. The world has a right to know about these little known delicacies.

COCONUT COURAGE

First: the account and tale of WWII 'coconut battlefield/beach front wine'. This drink was known by several different names - 'battlefield booze', 'battlefield beach booze', 'beachfront battle booze', and some even referred to it as 'coconut delight'. And yes, some soldiers even called this drink, 'coconut courage' for obvious reasons.

It seems that some thirsty American military men were fighting their nation's battles during WWII in the islands in the South Pacific war zone. Their officers deemed this a 'dry zone', i.e. 'no booze allowed'. However, unknown to them, this was about to change.

The American fighting man has long been known for his creativity and create was what several of them did.

First, the thirsty men noticed that there was a plentiful supply of coconuts most everywhere in these parts. They also knew that these coconuts contained some 'milk', or juice. Some of the soldiers from the southern parts of the USA knew how to make beverages from corn, etc., corn cob wine and more. So, they started by gathering coconuts, and making a small hole in them with a bayonet. Then they took the small sugar packets they had saved up from their c-rations, and from fellow soldiers, and poured sugar down into the coconuts.

After that step, they added water from their canteens, through the small hole, plugged up the hole with a small twig and shook the coconuts well to mix the ingredients.

Next, they would bury the coconuts in the sand of the hot tropical beach, taking care to place them above high tide mark. Of course the soldiers would mark these locations with sticks etc., so as not to lose them.

Every day they were in the same area, they would dig up the coconuts, and shake them well, then re-bury them. They knew that in the tropical heat, that in only a few days, they would have a 'spirited beverage', inside each coconut.

If the troops had to move due to battles or other reasons, many soldiers would dig up their precious special coconuts and move them with them.

Some of the officers did think that it was strange to see the men taking coconuts along, but reasoned that the men were probably worried that they might run short of food rations and didn't investigate.

In cases where the troops had moved before the special coconuts were ready to render their potent nectar, they would re-bury them in the new location. In a short time, officers started noticing their men acting strangely, and at times laughing and wildly running up and down the beach.

This was a battle zone, and often drew fire from the Japanese snipers, sometimes with bad results. The officers could see that these men appeared drunk but knew that they couldn't be, not in this 'dry zone' where booze was prohibited.

However, back on the beach, the contents of many coconuts were consumed by thirsty soldiers and marines. Thus, these drinks were called by various names, 'Battlefield Booze', 'Beachfront Booze', 'Coconut Delight', and even was called, 'Coconut Courage'. It was rumored that 'Coconut Courage' played a part in some of their battle successes.

It was also said, by some Japanese prisoners, that the Japanese soldiers could see that their US attackers were braver than normal, much like a 'banzai attack' at times! As well they noticed this more when the battle zone was littered with coconuts which had small holes carved in them.

It has long been known that courage can come from strange and varied places! No, I ain't done yet. Yes, another story of yet another exotic drink:

PUNKIN JACK

Here is a little story about a drink that sounds plumb scary, but is said to be 'frighteningly good'.

The following is the disgustingly true account of an exotic drink, aptly named, 'Punkin Jack'. This recipe originates in the poverty stricken coal fields of southern Indiana and is indeed different. Making 'Punkin Jack' is so simple that it's scary.

My friend, Larry, told it like this:

- Go out in the pumpkin patch and pick out one or more of the biggest, best pumpkins in the patch.
- Next step, take your pocketknife and carve out the top, or lid part of the pumpkin. Put the knife away, there's no more carving, you ain't making a jack-o-lantern!
- Next step, scoop out the pulp and seed from inside the pumpkin, however you can, just get 'er done.
- Then, the next step, when your momma ain't looking, is 'borrow' some sugar from her kitchen and sneak out.
- Then, next step, dump sugar down in the pumpkin, and add water 'til it's about half full.
- Next, carefully replace the pumpkin's lid that you had carved out.
- After this it's a good idea to mark the pumpkin so no one tries to take it and make a jack-o-lantern out of it.

I then asked Larry, "What's the next step?"
Larry replied, "When it's done, it's ready to drink."
Of course I asked, "Larry, how do you know when it's done?"
He answered, "Just watch the pumpkin, and after a couple of weeks or so it will

start to cave in, that's when you know it's done."

I then said, "So, then what do you do?"
Larry then said, "That's when you take the lid off the pumpkin, go get the water dipper, it's party-time."

He pointed out that as long as you get to the pumpkin before the lid caves in and lets the flies in, it's sanitary enough. Well, at least that's what he claims!

So, in relation to the making of 'Punkin Jack' story, I had an inspiration. Here is an excellent theme party idea; actually it might be considered 'the ultimate garden party'. I firmly believe this to be a Halloween original.

This account of 'Punkin Jack' is followed by a plan for a very different kind of garden party, which would work even better as a 'Halloween-themed' party. trick or treat, some pumpkins are the 'pumpkin jack treats, while others are traditional jack-o-lanterns.

For this Halloween party, masks or costumes are optional, because it's likely

that after a few dippers of 'Punkin Jack',
you wouldn't be able to recognize anyone
anyhow. Attendees must bring their own
lawn chair, or five gallon bucket, to sit on,
plus a clean, long handled dipper.
(Bringing a cup or glass is optional).

Some think that couples drinking from the
same container is very romantic.

This party takes some advance planning,
but it is definitely a one of a kind party.
This themed party could well bring new
importance to Halloween for adults.
Redneck trick or treat at its best!

This might be
a better use
for a 'punkin'
than
grandma's
traditional 'punkin' pie;
So live dangerously and give it a try.

A FINAL WORD OF CAUTION

Accept no substitutes; make sure you are getting genuine Kentucky corn cob wine. As well make sure that the wine has been hand crafted by authentic full-blooded Kentuckians, using the best traditional methods, in the best-known corn cob winemaking district in the world. Which are, of course, the beautiful fertile hills along the majestic Ohio River. Accept no substitutes, beware of imitations. Make sure the bottle, jug, or Mason® jar has the, 'Made in Kentucky' label.

Now that you have been thoroughly educated about the subtleties and nuances concerning this excellent beverage, consume it and enjoy it to the fullest.

Please drink responsibly and don't get hog drunk and make a damn fool out of yourself.

Around here drinking responsibly means holding the jug or jar with both hands. Get careless and you'll have to clean up the mess. As well this could lead to the necessity for an environmental spill cleanup!

Please don't try to imitate or copy our time-honored recipe for making Kentucky corn cob wine.

There ain't nuthin' much worse than a damn copycat!

ACKNOWLEDGEMENTS

We gratefully acknowledge the generosity of all those who helped in gathering these erroneous facts and misinformation, unfounded folklore, factually flawed statements, and just plain 'hillbilly tales' for this publication.

We thank you, one and all for your creativity, and story embellishments. We thank you, one and all, for your unselfishly sharing of these. While it is widely understood that many facts and tales are embellished and grow with each re-telling, some of these are indeed 'whoppers'.

Also thanks to 'the corn cob winos society of Kentucky'. As well, we thank them for inviting us to their 'wine tastins', and 'wine drinkins'. As long as civilized society continues to have cultural events of this magnitude one can be sure that the future of our country and it's wine culture is assured and in good hands.

As well, culturally, we Americans will continue to be world leaders. These events are always a high point for us. Yes, a truly high point.

To those reviewers who made snotty references to this book, here is my response:

It should be noted that some book reviewers and critics make crude and insensitive remarks about authors. I would like to take this opportunity to respond to some of these, here and now!

One unnamed, but well known critic said, "I think this book was written by a common drunk." In response to that unwarranted criticism I would like to say, "I resent being referred to as being common."

Another facetious critic said, and I quote, "Obviously the author of the book 'The Kentucky Corn Cob Wine Connoisseur' is the result of our public school's policy of 'no child left behind'". To that unkind remark, I would like to say, "I graduated from the eighth grade with all the rest. Feel free to check my credentials."

Yet another self-ordained critic said, "the contents of this book are plain lies." To this I would like to say, "Sir, there is nothing plain about these lies."

To the snotty reviewer who said this book was nothing less than a criminal misuse of pen and paper and the English language, I say, "Sir, I'll write the books,

you go on back to writing on restroom walls, and don't forget your crayons."

Other books, e-books, and audio books from Jim Hubler at Amazon.com and Barnes & Noble

The Cliffs of Leavenworth
Some Trucking Tales (Volume 1)
A Collection of Comic Satirical Poetry

And don't miss Jim's music available on CDs, DVDs, and mp3 format from Amazon.com and cdbaby.com

Mud Slinging USA, Volumes 1,2 &3
Pet A Dog ~ Help A Dog
Ballad of a Diesel Doctor
Boy, I've Backed A Rig More Miles
Trucking Between The Tracks
Beer, Cheaper Than Gas
I Ain't Worried About Retirement
The Devil's Convoy
Beginner's Luck

ABOUT THE AUTHOR

Jim Hubler (William James Hubler Jr.) is a former Hoosier, now living in Kentucky along the beautiful Ohio River. After many years as a Trucker who played in Country Bands on the weekends, he is now retired and doing what he always wanted to do - write.

He has been writing songs for many years, now he has recorded several of them, with the help of some very talented friends. A few years ago he started writing his first book, and now has written three, with more in the works, and coming soon. As well, he writes some Poetry, 'Part-time Poet', thus this book.

Jim's interests are many and varied. He likes dogs, big trucks, good guitars, and writes about everything he likes, plus more. He loves the humorous side of life, but also writes some things 'as serious as a heart attack'. His main rule of life is, "Never Trust A Man That Don't Like Dogs."